73

Heirloom

ℭ

by Ashia S Ajani

Write Bloody Publishing

writebloody.com

First edition.
ISBN: 9781949342499

Cover Design by Alejandro Baigorri
Interior Layout by Nikki Steele
Edited by Blythe Baird
Proofread by Sam Preminger
Author Photo by [Name]

Type set in Bergamo.

Printed in the USA

Write Bloody Publishing
Los Angeles, CA

Support Independent Presses
writebloody.com

For Ella.

Heirloom

Heirloom

I.
EXODUS

II.
FLOOD

III.
THIRST

IV.
REBIRTH

"I had no nation now but the imagination" —Derek Walcott,
"The Schooner Flight"

"I'm a planet, you a local bitch." —BbyMutha, "Sailor Goon"

I.
EXODUS

CREATION STORY

in the beginning, there was my greatmother & my greatmother's stock pot. its capacious abyss brothing. a fist emerged first, then a heartbeat. the men bubbled from it unscathed. a gxrl emerged spitting soap from their lips. we all sprung forth steeped in culture, the soft fat of ancestry clinging to granny's good broth.

my ancestors laughed in the faces of white Gods. my ancestors were brave. some were cowards. some became cruel in their apathy. some mistook the white cassava flesh of their palms as transcendence. my ancestors survived; the only wound that mattered. my people organized. got blamed for doing it poorly. got blamed for doing it well. got blamed for misspells. their own deaths. had our history ripped from our tongues & fed back to us, sterilized.

we made tough choices. we took jobs in factories working to extract & distill natural resources into unrecognizable fuel, until we too became unrecognizable.

we got cancer from working in sludge. bone disease. emphysema. we lived on toxic land. we got our land seized. we seized land. we didn't get treatment. we didn't get monetary compensation. sometimes they made documentaries about it. about us. awareness is the best we could hope for.

sometimes we laughed because we deserved to, & Lord knows we needed it. some of us had cookouts. some of us played spades. some of us got to second base under the pine trees in the backyard with the boy with a mouth full of metal. some of us smoked herb. some of us didn't want to get our hair wet. some of us dried out, ya dig? some of us danced, danced, danced until we sweated out that liquor. then all that was left was to return to memory.

some of us grew gardens. some of us walked barefoot on damp soil. some of us grew our hair long & loc'ed. some of us raised healers. too many of us needed healing. some of us gossiped. became grandmas & aunties. stirred our own soup pots. respirited the cauldron. kept each other close.

at the end, there was darkness. & no light could slice through it, it was meant to hold the everything of all things, & thus it was safe. the word came, & the word was Black & good & bountiful, & thus it was safe. creatures of biblical proportions, new gods lept from the abyss, a wide open womb brought forth Black earth, & thus it was safe, was all guarded, all gatekept, all sweet soil cascading into oblivion. that oblivion, a Black bruise mending the smacked around earth, even the dust it left behind was kept safe. even as we watched the midnight sky fall from its heavenly border, we were kept safe. in the wet. in the sorrow. in the quiet space. in all that blood & turmoil. every dusk swept day i thank a Black woman's rage for ensuring my survival.

LANDFILL

In the morning, the ghosts are listless.
The world goes quiet without preamble,
pray to all the gods who look like me
and to the ones who don't.
Even the faceless deities have a place here.
Grocery bags fossilized into quilt, cough drop wrappers,
a tooth;
all organs built of silicone and rupture.
A menstrual cup (pretend used for three years prior)
croons its tongueless lullaby alongside
saran wrap stained auburn with turmeric and grease,
carved out belly fat, //neon razors, bloody underwear,
a pinch of his pubic hair.
Acrylic nails compete with bits of skin and cartilage
[how do you save smoke?]
—a testament to ancestors worn
and discarded like scraps of cloth.
Headless baby doll & twelve used condoms,
broken brassieres that remind me of my ex-girlfriend.
God knows how many broken combs, brushes,
picks pluck permanence
in this brown-green slime.
Prescription pill bottles my mother says not to dispose of in this
way.
Nothing dies here. That is the purpose
of stuffing a landscape full of rubbish.
Objects are only relevant in terms of their circulation.
Everything has an origin: maybe that
doesn't mean as much as we would like it to mean.

SOUTHERN SYMPHONY IN FOUR MOVEMENTS

blue in green
    1) the overwhelming feeling of melancholy when you should
    be happy
    2) sadness & jealousy felt at the loss of a lover to another
    person
    3) the third tune on miles davis' 1959 album, Kind of Blue

    I.
and when the people in the backwoods
                            breathed, amen echoed
              through the trees.
combing a strong vibrato through those ancient green fros, the
cicadas
joined their verdant cousins drenched in praise, carried beyond
                        the pulpit. the wood that raised

the church,
shorn skin of sistren ax-felled, a sort of revenge for its complicity
in the black curtain it made of our ancestors.
surely we can't blame the trees:
how easy we make a prayer out of pain,
a tall oak out of acorn,
isn't that the point of praise? to find the mighty in the minute?
to marvel at how even the cicadas express their desire through
song?

    II.
there is nothing like midnight music to shake a few leaves from
the soul,
even when the soul itself is trapped in limbo, evergreen.
Miles, I too miss the chords striking through the forest,
though I know we have built fragile nests
in this hell & will protect our songbird youth
no matter the consequence.
                    Miles, when a New York City cop split
your pharaoh's nose like the Red Sea,
did the song that spilled out of you
become lost to Northern diplomacy?
when the blood stained your pressed white shirt, the onlookers
standing by snapping pictures

did it remind you of those postcards that made the South a
spectacle?

III.
God was exhausted with creation, so He founded the dark to hold
every dream

                                    deferred & peace,
of course, was one of those
dreams defeated. so we leaned on hallelujahs rooting
through damp undergrowth to guide our hearts
back to good graces.
languid vernacular tall as cypress, heavily wooded,
standing guard against colonial teeth. we could live down here,
again.
the face of an emergent South cascading through the pine,
buttressed by memory.

IV.
some days I wish we could return to the original gospel of the
poplars,
          to sing with the barking tree frog,
                    the beetle,
                    the short-eared owl,
the souls still trapped in the branches
         —a kind of evening blue,
                        a kind of blue

in green

COLLARDS

The pot stays on. On the stove, the simmer sojourns south.
Hunger don't have no place in this kitchen. In this kitchen, every
Black belly has its feed.

This ornamental garden tastes best after the first frost. After what
could not survive falls to decay in service of more sumptuous
fruit.

O, my clever, sour Gods smoked from brine and whimsy,
sweetwater recalls me a Mississippi mad woman. Sick to the soul
with all this fruit. Yearning for

                                    what it means to feed
                                    & be fed.

GOD SAVE THE FOREST

I didn't intentionally spurn the forest,
rather
it became another question of Southern belonging
I didn't have the patience to unravel.

Must've been when the little white kids next door
asked if we wanted to play "Cowboys and Indians" —
all I could think about was the split
in my conquered DNA that stood on both
ends of the chastening rod.

Or maybe when a man held a shotgun to the back of
a good man's head while we were out in the field,
asked: *whose land you think you on, boy?*
Neither of ours.
We just learned to love it because it was the only thing that
granted us some semblance of peace.

Cousin says he has encountered poisonous snakes
in the Panamanian jungle, & this scared him less than doing
research in the deep South.
Snakes are usually more frightened by you than you are of them
same goes for white folks but Lord,
how I prefer a fang to those trigger fingers.

I didn't intentionally spurn the darkness until they
claimed ownership of that which once sheltered us.

When all that was hunt & run soaked my endings in bloodlust
through this violent cat & mouse condition—
the inherent trickery of my blood begged me to stay grounded
when all I could imagine was flight.
The voices in these woodlands are alive with vengeance.

Maybe this is why white people fear the dark and what it holds.
We marvel at its ability to hold,
call it semantics, a cultural linguistic loophole,
our right to something.

Abuela weaves together sweet tales about the backwoods that
were once hers.
Long after the plantation manifestation made a mockery of her
inheritance,
the trees held their secrets with rope and flame.
I can't help but envision my abuela laughing,
running not from any one thing
but towards the witching hour our foremothers once found
refuge in.

Mississippi is a graveyard of all my kin's wildest ambitions.
We play pretended Americanness until it felt real enough
to sink into,
until it didn't defend us from the light,
until the Superfund affliction reminded us of the well-earned
savagery in our marrow.

I flee from what my ancients trusted, & isn't that the most
heart-wrenching betrayal of my blood
—to deny myself access to the Blackest parts of this earth?

My great-great-great-grandmother's phantom footsteps litter the
ground like dead leaves.
Lineage always returns to an ill-understood trauma of existing in
between shadow & soul.

What is the difference between haunting & protecting a place?
Is it one of volition?
The wounds down here are older than the flesh that displaced
them,
but the twilight reminds me that we could feel whole yet.

Black people in the South breathe life into dark and call it home:
Black as the soil that birthed bright cotton,
this Mississippi Delta madness. Home:
this wild, expansive Blackness. Home:

Mississippi, baby, on my good days I imagine you soft, lazy-
draped in gracious green, sacred darkness
cradling all that unloved Black.

ORCHIDS AS A METAPHOR FOR DIASPORIC ANGST

My mother tells me a story: in the early years of her practice, a
white lady specifically requested that my mother perform her
surgery because she knew "Black people aren't allowed to make
mistakes." She would've died for this perfection & compelled my
mother to do the same.

The point was never to avoid rot. Rot comes, an unannounced
funeral procession, slow & deliberate. All the blossom remembers
is what it meant to be well prior to its fall. Roots washed clean
with peroxide, soft, watery lesions of bacterial brown spots made
plain that something, somewhere went wrong. MSNBC stays on.
The TV crackles, coughs and spews its bad news, its own black
hearse rickety round-tripped into the warm interior of a body
already in decline.

In spite of disharmony, or perhaps because of it, my mother puts
her latex enshrined fingers in warm, brown soil. Manipulates
radices, lifeblood & leaf, retrieves breath. Of course my mother
would choose the most difficult plants to rear—dancing lady,
slipper, dendrobium. Delicate names for delicate plants. Some
plants will bloom purely out of genetic propensity. Orchids,
however, can propagate without flowering, & herein lies the myth
of frailty. If you don't recreate the conditions necessary for
fluorescence, they'll say 'forget you' & won't flower. I can live here,
a precarious life, but I won't give you the promise of petals.

Mother's palms know this stubborn tissue well. All too familiar,
these intricate capillaries, a diversity that is so vast one could study
it for a lifetime & still never learn a fraction of it, would like to
remain unknown. My mother has a surgeon's hands, steady &
steadfast, performing vivisection, eager to know these roots.

But even when the roots take, only a few flower in the dry plains
of Denver, compared to their tropical origins. Terrifyingly
beautiful simply in utterance, in what could be if these conditions
were ideal. Beseeching still: does the soil carry the scent of my
blood?

These petals forever en reve, combative, as if it did not fruit from a
tree of rage, an epiphytic extension of grief plucked from bark.

A BLACK HAIR STUDY IN COMMENSALISM, I.E. GREASE AND GLORY IN THE MARSHLANDS OF MY SCALP

sit still, knees dig into small shoulders
seating me steady
as my grandmother's raisined fingers
grease the chitlin circuit of my scalp
singing soft bayou hymns: *you're safe here.*
if i could maroon into the forest of my hair
i would: no questions asked,
no notebooks left behind, unspoiled.
Restore me back better, fill my knocked
around head with box braids
reminiscent of Mississippi cypress
against a swamp of salty skin.
This overgrown railroad of twist & coil
rejects the dirty promise of industry,
the dust & rust honeyed into fertilizer
where an insurgent bloom can emerge
                                    evergreen.

here, there is no clank of metal
no concrete coffins covering my most
authentic kinkycurl iterations as memory
begs my safe return.
any shoreline edge erosion

is my responsibility & mine alone;
the fuzz of new growth, an aerophytic marvel
marking tendrils territory for dispersal &
arrives with the wind, wind, rush.
the naps at my kitchen signal the season's
emergent abundance. untamed
kanekalon bundles
irritate me into length retention—
this veneration we make to protect
our best selves

            & let our treetops seduce
            success under the golden sun.

DEVIL'S PUNCHBOWL (NATCHEZ, MS)

in the span of one year following the Civil War, over 20,000 Black people were starved and left for dead in the concentration camp called the Devil's Punchbowl. wild peach trees sprung up from the resulting mass grave.

the
ruby-throated
hummingbird is the most
common hummingbird that roosts
in the Great River state. at the dawn of wild
peach season, their scarlet breasts swell with carnal lust.
on rare occasion, hummingbirds will craft their nests & lay
their eggs on a peach. sheltered under green laced shade,

camouflage threaded from plant down & spider silk hangs heavy
with life's viscous nectar. Genesis dictates God responsible for
this ambrosia, a stone fruit salvation sent from heaven.

existence is by its nature precarious: we all dissolve into precarity,
occupying our minds with whatever sweet, honeyed thing offers
its body as a refuge. slice through fuzzy, vulnerable flesh to
exhume a hardened heart-stone from tender pulp here.
fruit falls untouched. the blossoms of deep spring
been trickled down to soil's dark grave ad
infinitum anticipating harvest. that
summer, antebellum spirits
will crush tiny bones
underfoot. trees
weep nectar
again.

DRAPETOMANIA

*"a form of mania supposedly affecting slaves in the 19th century,
manifested by an uncontrollable impulse to wander or run away
from their white masters, preventable by regular whipping. The
disorder was first identified in a medical report that is often cited as
a fanciful case of psychologism"* —Oxford English Dictionary

often, i dream of flight.
this makes me susceptible to any
gin-stinking wisdom that comes
my way—

better days are coming.
the drunkards on the corner blow
kisses masked by hiccupped
vengeance, eyes soot-dark
with visions of marronage.
"why you ain't smiling?
you blessed my nigga" says the man
at the city bus stop.
instinctively, my wings unfurl.
perhaps it's just the smell of last night's dinner
lingering on his coat,
good feed enticing wayward flock,
but there are always unnamed hungers who
draw us closer to truthsayers;

Lord, i been starving.

stuck in the oil slick, plumage clipped.
eager to find its destination happy,
a patient violence lives at the base of my spine.
desire stands guard against colonial teeth,
says, *"run."*
i oblige,
exposing the geography of hurt
across these United States.

RUNNING
for Ahmaud Arbery (1994-2020). Rest in Power.

Once again, I return to the outdoors in search of cleaner breath.
My lungs, a peripatetic duo foraging for whatever fills,
collapses or relieves. In the South, breath is heavy. Humid
palpitations mark this flesh ripe for taking. This exhalation
is not cheap. The flight in these legs, a vestigial burden passed
down generations of restlessness. We stay moving—it is harder
to kill a thing in constant motion.
I say no names for fear I will summon something wicked.
I do not look at what hunts me. Rather, I embrace the freedom
of exodus. When one of Us runs, the rest follow. It is an unspoken
bond of reluctant prey. You would think with everyone trapped
in they houses, the predators would take a break. Even Jesus got
one day of rest. Two bullets hunt & run behind me. The asphalt
loves this body too much for return. Whiteness rewrites my
breath into blood. Into ash. Self-deputized by whatever golden
emanations they deem worthy of judgment, these violent beasts
reclaim open space that was never theirs to covet. My feet shift
with a sole desire to mind my business & keep. it. pushing. My
heart, a rustle in the wilderness sought for horrific consumption.
I do not want to be surveilled. I just want to feel the cool air
wrapped around my Black body & for once, feel free to exhale.

A BODY'S BEST DEFENSE AGAINST PARASITISM, A.K.A. IMMOVABLE DECOMPOSER

"the dead are growing under the living" —Jean Metellus

each day begs a new amnesia.
                    the ghosts, the griefs, violent in their indulgences,
drink to bloodwine ruin & wealth.

in turn, i observe
the flea, the leech, the blowfly that nourishes
itself with another's suffering.

yes you, you scavenger, you empty headed consumer,
you hit your head & never recovered, you (turkey) vulture,
you gutless glutton,
                    how i despise you.

the stink of crucifixion lingers in your sheets; i mourn the
flightless souls felled to death amidst the silk and sorrow of your
most tenacious seduction.

in dust, i remain prisoner to the laboratory,
sequestered in manila humus
—here lies the unnamed, the unknown, the *Black*.
the anthropologist & the social worker seek to make the negro
human.
                    the teacher, the oncologist, the art curator
                    define a body beyond its own terminology,

                    cut a cord to culture, purge muscle memory
until what remains is atrophied.
under such conditions the negro does not blossom, does not fruit.
instead, the negro chews at the root; a decomposer
breaks down what was laid to waste,
like sunbeams splitting dust into prisms, i expose the dirty &
let it pass through me.

i spoil what is already prone to rot
a mycelial vagrancy, ungovernable.
god buried me in the ground to root & root
i may,

                   a greedy heterotroph.   sorry cuz, you

can't quite get rid of me.

IN THE THICKET

"weeds are flowers" —George Washington Carver

in white imagination, Black folks exist as entertainers or
boogeymen. like my grandmother, i wish to make a mean life of
both tar baby & briar patch. at once the same, occasionally one or
the other. somewhere between fascination & fetishization lies the
shapeshifter's gift.

girlboi speaks their fragmented speech & the chatter of gulls
knocked clean from sky echoes. someone(s) once said i need to
culture my tongue so i turned to the wisdom of evening bats,
erudite in their echolocation. my mouth twists in praise-laden
mimicry of another in-between species.

behind the loose bark of whatever forest remains, or sheltered by
blackberry vine (its unwelcoming claws a demarcation against
encroachment), weeds overtake granny's plot long before a white
man can move his fence a few inches every summer. prickly bodies
hide man-made borders.

we are, after all, connected by our bitter rooted histories,
the same strange flower emerging, year after year from bulbs of
empire, poisonous with their long memories. some things are just
Black folks' business. the rest, a fable.

II.
FLOOD

I STILL WON'T GET MY HAIR WET

the cold water will swallow you whole, chile
& where will you be without this landlocked abandon?

gramma chides when i venture a new baptism;
she snaps on my swim cap tight enough to knock these
perm-bruised edges loose. the chlorine clean makes it pure enough

for plunge. my lungs fill with chemicals.
we buy back our health, a purloined possession.
this kind of thirst summons an ancient lust.

we been parched for centuries. in secret, i seek to swim,
cloaked by what carried & buried my bloodline.
i am hotblooded, overeager to splash & cool off.

growing up in Colorado, i never was a water-connected person.
besides, my bloodline lacks proclivity towards moisture,
though these lungs know nothing but flood.

years ago, in the wild edges of Missouri,
my paternal grandfather throws my adolescent father
into Smithville Lake, shouts *Swim.*

if they come for you, you gotta know how to float
if they come for you, you better hold your goddamn breath.

HEIRLOOM

listen, i know that the empire has   crooked teeth. they
won't save me, but at the very least
could cut through my gratitude cloth.
they could tell me i look pretty *once*   i
become undone with sorrow
as i undress my best selves
        for the sake of self-preservation;
the skirt woven from my great-auntie's
mirror. i held back coal-streaked
tears while a man with a degree sought   pity.
now, sullied fabric wraps
my wounds soot-stained. a ghost dollar   rises
from the ashes, becomes
placeholder for peace; grief swings from   my
branches dropping threads of
oil stained lineage. ghostly, i release
        string from mankind's cruel   fibers,
the fabric of me; unravel the stillness   that
gives way to desire. even
in my quiet moments i crave [affirmation].
perennial fire shorn from progress; at
dawn i take the bus with   other
folks on their way to walk
their own bed of coals, prepping   their
soles for the mean heat of a gray living.
maybe i dance, do a   jive
something just to stay alive—
one day, i'll drape the world   over
my shoulder and run with it.
say, i loved it, i washed it, i lived   in it
long enough to feel its sting.

MY PHONE AUTOCORRECTS "THANK YOU" TO "THANK GOD"

auntie affirmations of a boi venus after they post a pic on
facebook begin as follows:

ALL CAPS! SMOOCHES

MAY GOD CONTINUE TO BLESS YOU

                                        AND YOUR

DREAMS (my gender is Black)

                        ALWAYS

PROTECT YOUR JOY (womanhood is the only hood i ran
from)

                                        AS YOU
                                        PURSUE YOUR
                                        GOALS (girldom
                                                seldom
                                                satisfied, but
                                                it was from
                                                that seed i
                                                sprung forth)
HI ANGEL

                                YOU HAVE THAT IVERA

[YOUR G-MA, RIP] LOOK

                KEEP LOVING
NATURE (jolly green giantess unyellowed)

                ENJOY   EACH
MOMENT (look at how they ungender the self)

        I'M SO PROUD OF YOU (:   BEAUTY   AT
ITS BEST

GIVE 'EM

                                              HELL &
                                              FREE (tired
                                              of being the
                                              baddest,
                                                        most
                                              vicious bitch)

THE LAND (spellcast my sorrows into new growth)

                                 YOU ARE STUNNING
OPEN UP THOSE BEAUTIFUL EYES

GORGEOUS (finally i realize what it means for the divine in me)

BREAKING GENERATIONAL CURSES (to recognize the
divine in you)

                                          I AM
WITH YOU IN SPIRIT (to be seen as a heavenly vessel for all
that God embodies)

                GREAT-MOTHER IS CELEBRATING IN THE HEAVENS
                FOR YOU

STAY SAFE (to revel that the site of you is

                                          all that's
                                          needed to
                                          walk among
                                          beauty)

LOVE YOU
LOVE YOU
LOVE YOU

                  GIVE ME A CALL
                  WHEN YOU GET A CHANCE

OCEAN SONG

"natural disaster." Lord please, break this lie at the [radical].

what is natural about prolonged neglect? what is natural about disaster cycling?

i do not fear apocalypse—that is your guilt-ridden worry. you can't kill an already zombified thing.

i rebuke your pleas for forgiveness—when a young boy who swallowed sea water instead of freedom pens his death inevitable, i have no time to expunge records.

yes, i am livid. i have too much hate in my blood to let go and let God.

we need bodies, but the Lost Ones linger purgatory amongst our ranks.

the waves arrived. by nature, took everything they could carry—family photo albums, telephone poles, tethered bodies washed clean, any sense of false permanence meant to ground.

when the sea swallowed houses whole, drowned entire prisons in salt, the island didn't beat its head against the waves instead, she bent her spine enough to awaken a latent grief filled to brim with

insurgent restoration, called us kin & offered a storm to weather our meanest hurt.

we live steady with lapsed wounds in search of wilder flesh. if purification is our birthright, why then are we forced to carry a muddied agony recycling its wounds around and round again?

nothing came easy.

the earth, inflamed & vengeful, never begged. she bellowed her hurt, pulled her heart across the Atlantic, hurled a warning, & another, another shattered fragment of calluses shorn silky, her teething tendrils forming a carefully curated bedlam.

like everything born of motion, spirit will return, time immemorial. return to brackish water, to a jeweled darkness. a forever reminder of what you wished to drown, how instead, we reclaimed these sweet lungs for swim.

THE PLUG WON'T
after Mykki Blanco

i grease myself with lipgloss & lotion
perhaps a lil blush will conjure color courage
to go sit in this nigga's honda for the third time
in two weeks.
the weedman is the only man to ever see me
with my scarf on. i dip & toe a green line. the
intimacy of purchase lingers want on my lips.
yes, this too is heady. in the eveningtime, i
upcycle heartbreak, try on a new facade of
sexycool meant to bring back bliss. eyes low
i coax memory to rewrite itself through a wrapped
fatty & weighty conversations like

did you know so n' so died?

$\qquad\qquad\qquad$ *ash fell from the sky when—*

$\qquad\qquad\qquad\qquad\qquad\qquad\qquad\qquad\qquad$ *he*

$\qquad\qquad\qquad\qquad\qquad\qquad\qquad$ *didn't*

$\qquad\qquad\qquad\qquad\qquad\qquad\qquad$ *deserve—*

the doctor says— $\qquad$ *rent is up another 175 so let*

$\qquad\qquad\qquad\qquad\qquad\qquad\qquad$ *me get*

$\qquad\qquad\qquad\qquad\qquad$ *a 1/2 ounce of anything*

that will pull my mind
back from the brink of no return. eager to oblige,
weedman hands me a bag of indigo to evince

a night sky from beyond my wildest emptiness.
both of us Black & hustling, rife with dreams
of soulmates evergreen. this be an elegiac alliance.
heartache notwithstanding, he beholds my blessings
everlasting. lovers come & go but this—this is
something sacred. i don't know where my paycheck ends
& his begins, but i love (the idea of) being tethered to
something. i am a shapeshifter eroded by grief;
render my tenement hollow, let the fullness of me
idle below an unseeded frontier to conquer.
i call myself a Before. simply ungrounded.
how i began? not like this.

SUNSET//STORM//RISE//REPEAT

with the same seductive fervor of budding romance clay stained
wind ran rosy rings 'round my heatlust face pushed me towards
akimbo legs of springtime plucked my peach blossoms clean
nestled against a sunset splayed across the nighttime sky
anticipated by streaks of vermillion new waves of scarlet envy
emerge from my flushed flesh in pursuit of your most carnal color
i dip my reds with my lover's oranges with their soft dissolving
precious caverns in my teeth where memory will exist after first, i
was desire shame came later once i became lost in the blush of it all
caught up in cardinal touch everlasting bursts of greedy guts split
watermelon red fell from starched bedsheets a vibrant sacrifice
spilled sweet color in pursuit of color call me color4color i
demand the whole sunstorm of you shower me in flamboyant
streaks of nectar hook me like the pale pink mouths of fishes we
will fry later loosen my tightly spun braids glass unbeaded kiss my
sunburnt scalp til the cherrywine evening sings us into another
iteration of godly replant me in red earth red earth red earth teach
me the rubescent secret of your burning touch

SHUCKING OYSTERS ON THE ATLANTIC COAST

hand shucks oyster
              steals. sharpens
heavy hand leaden fingers
palm spun
      detangles
             pearl unsheathed.

tongue twisted
      story told
            sweetened. sad
god. golden & ghastly
      rigorous survival
            shortened.

knife seasoned
          unlocked.
ocean salt wept
          unborn
              taste
purified. water clarified
          labor

unheeded.

pull
          flesh to your
          lips & marvel
                  at
the flavor of
             what persists &
          still tongues
a soft
          existence

MEDITATIONS ON SWEETNESS AND OTHER FRUITS

my mother asks the pronouns of my crush
as a courtesy, knowing which one she prefers.
this gives her hope, girlchildren to aspire to.
nevertheless a persistent stinging, ringing
smoke above the vibrations of the words we
speak to one another. i don't kiss using the same
tongue i confess in, my teeth always chattering
away a girlhood dispossessed.
always remember: she the accommodating one.
i basketcase know-it-all split between all divinity, fully spatcocked
over glowing coals; i expose my beating muscle to the flame
and the flame, of course, doesn't hold the salt of me,
doesn't cook the meat into anything tender.
ain't no thang cut muscle deeper than a Black mother's refusal.
i an expensive lesson in expectation—gluttonous
in my shameful desire.
i confess, i prefer fruit.
in the eveningtime, when the heat becomes bearable,
my eyes set on the horizon, twisted with visions of
watermelon women tonguing their signatures across
my inner thighs, the flavor of kumquats descending from my
lover's lips.
true, i am greedy.
summer arrives with its ephemeral jewels;
succulent peaches, bountiful berries short-lived
freedom ends at the corner of my lip, lest what i
love begs to remain at the border of burning.
with the scent of honeysuckle in my hair
a boi drenched in fallen flowers ripens me ready,
drunk with plum wine, the mere
promise of nectar enough to satisfy a whole
darkness of longing. the slow roast of time
descends on all of us, but for this moment i
live between a fresh kill & a blossoming tree.
no matter. it all matters.
light the joint &
exhale your juicy transgressions into my eager mouth.

GROUNDWATER GODS

despite their affinity for land living, pillbugs are more closely
related to crustaceans than crickets or ladybugs. perhaps this is
why they burrow in a garden's moist afterlife,
crawling through the decomposing roots of our namesake.

when i was a child, i would pull open dead logs and rocks
searching for these miniature archivists, doctors stitching together
stories of soil between what greed poisoned its dark body.
torturous as it was, i turned them over on their backs to see if sky
could illuminate

> their gray-black torsos. i wanted to
> inhabit a shadowed underbelly too
> eager to find solace in the veil of
> existence. instead, they guarded their
> wisdom, curled up into an armored ball
> at the first show of sun.

i've always thought this instinct manifested from fear, yet biology
reminds us fear is a placeholder for protection: a vestigial longing
bounded by drought & the storm that follows
soon after. *sweet underworld deities, alchemists bewitched by a
surface level damnation—*

> *lend me your insurgency. teach me how to*
straddle two different worlds
> *each damning your capaciousness. in the*
slippages between heaven &
> *hell, you filter out the bad & remind us*
> *what goodness can still be upheld.*

ODE TO THE SPIRIT OF LEFT EYE

looking down a waterfall in La Ceiba,
Left Eye, nude & alive uttered:
when i was a kid, i wished all this.
i can't help but tease out the irony
in getting all you ever wanted mere days
before your spirit quits this earth. the devil
inside, subdued for the time being. the tongue
forks. two paths: flames or flight.
maybe it was those different personalities
begging to be released from a constricting
vessel, Gemini that she was, never
satiated by what could be obtained,
always fascinated with the beyond, the crass,
the unexplainable aching within us all. one
twin holds the torch, the other follows close
behind with the watering can. i could
slash & burn my woes or drown them.
i could quench the soil's december thirst
after the land had been metamorphosed
through a brutal fire season. i can say
sorry from the same cheek i spit my venom.
i am afraid i have already lost what is
most dear to me & can never retrieve it.
i promise you, if i could isolate
the nucleus of my pain i would pluck
the disease from its root then bury it.
even as Left Eye watched a house
consumed in a conflagration of her own
creation, she couldn't placate the
parts of her that wanted to go down with the wreckage.
a penchant for flight burns deep
in our shared spirits.
as she held the leather soles of another
lopez, these wild premonitions of departure
etched want in her flesh. i, too, see dangerous
things & try to pay them no mind.
you give power to a thing when you
name it, so i wander aimlessly, ripping
titles from the haints that follow me.

BLACKEST BLUE
after Idiacanthus antrostomus, *the pacific blackdragon*

imagine, beyond the crest of some sailboat sunken to depth
                                 fishkin of prophetic proportions
gloat gleeful praise of ships saddled to sand.
yes, godless, rolling in the prestige of camouflage,
the sheen of soulful medicine that glistens in fins
too dark in depth to hold any light body.
                                          my mother talks to fish;
she sings to them open mouthed and gully lipped
observes their slender enciphered movements
dares to make fantasy about their splendid magic.
she is no stranger to making stealth survival.
                                    this bitter marronage,
burdened bliss of exile—the ocean floor remembers
every bone & nail that pried freedom from a rotted
floorboard.
monsters made sacred live
                        down
                              here.
in satisfaction, its magnificent depths unearthed,
inundated in bejeweled splendor, recall the eulogized
pleas for deliverance back eastward. these new bodies
make room for a rebirthed migration built of desire, not demand.
these spirits flitter between planes of scale & skin,
souls tethered in a shared sense of melanin
                                at last, deep sea cosmologies.
                                mother says, *let them breathe.*

NAMELESS

At coffee shops, I take on a new baptism. I just want my
cold brew. The jumbled pieces of genealogy settle into
old dust. Seeds knocked from my braids long, long ago.
My ancestry, choking on seawater. Lost, phonetically
abandoned. Softened cheekbones. Facing eastward. Always.
Any time some variation of my name is uttered, a dead
slave rises from behind my ear & pinches the skin red.
At the border between Zambia & South Africa: fresh.
Someone pronounces my name correctly for the first time.
All that is left in the space bounded by home & history
is longing. The hyphen between African-American. Super-
imposed identity. I surrender a piece of my body every
time I am asked to place root. Interesting enough to inquire.
All the mistakes of the Atlantic reside on my face. Nameless.
I'm sorry, I don't have any clean answers for you.

I think the Blackest thing about me
are my eyes.
Bless how they were taught to keep moving.
To seek truth.
To always greet the dawn with devotion.

III.
THIRST

DURAG

Forward moving, we always turn back
time. Like ocean, built of body, memory

(the God of good grease) paints follicles holy
and those waves, Lord, those ancient waves

facilitate a brother's boldest baptism, wipe me
down, a litany of all the good that came to stay.

The Atlantic remembers every part of Black
anatomy. Like a curse, a calling: those cold waters

shift & stagnate under a cotton polyester blend.
They never got to lay claim to the water, but by God

How they dam(n)ed, privatized, seized, overfished,
extracted, deregulated, poisoned, commodified,

pulled the cloth from the crease quick, like a run in
a stocking. Ripped the color clean from scalp—

an instantaneous divide reminds what can be taken
& what can be absolved.

Later, a Black boy will fit his mouth around the word 'rage',
hold it behind his tongue, ferment his brooding into savagery.

Watch him pull bones from the riverbed, casting wide
mesh drenched in cotton coagulations. Pray for summer rain

to rinse all these triflin' transgressions clean. Any flood breaks
a bullet's back, but does not siphon the blood back into body.

Baby, I can't help but enshrine you as a vengeful sea god—
drowning in all that drip, all that wet, all that sheen.

HOW THE DESERT GOT ITS CACTUS

after Sandra Cisneros

Before you became a cactus, you were a seed;
black & dainty. You were a field of possibility
under a moonlit sky. You were the sky. You were
the joint tucked behind the pretty boy's ears.
The tattooed knuckles I longed to kiss. T. R. U.
S. T. You were the soft tufts of fur in el viejo's
ears. The lime juice covering pungent cloves of
garlic auntie used to boil for maladies from
earaches to the flu.

So when you learned sorrow, you were shaken, as
though someone took a storm cloud & strung
you up with it. Put it in your midday tea, let it
simmer. You were bitter dandelion. You were
messy. But we both are, so it's ok. Sometimes.

Baby told me a story about the armadillo.
Painted a red summer on my cheek & told me to
laugh, to take my medicine. You were Colfax,
home to the chin & the boot that left its mark.
You were chicken bone & coyote. Left to lasso
the mountains & died up there.

Flowers grow on your thick limbs. Crucifix of
the desert, transpire our dusty transgressions.
Clay-stained scripture pours out of you in place
of rainfall. Goodness, gracious, amen.

AFTER MY SHOE SPREADS THE GUTS OF AN UNASSUMING EARTHWORM ACROSS A CROSSWALK DIDN'T IT JUST WANT TO BREATHE DIDN'T IT JUST WANT TO DANCE IN THE RAIN TOO

A body can be a prison if you let it.
Fanon calls a puddle an ecosystem minutes before a boot
disperses its wet contents. Split tongues emerge from the
fragments, eager to taste what lingers on the sole.

Power is the difference. This is a food chain, after all,
begging us to spin sustenance from scarce dew droplets.
Dark, wet continents fall from our hips, waiting to be caged
once the dust settles.

Small pond, small body, it must be so heartbreaking to
see yourself reflected in every iris that passes you over;
a well of emotion, motionless til the heat of summer
evaporates you into the invisible everythingness that surrounds us.

Just as the dehydrated hips of hibiscus widened
when met with moisture, so too shall you unfold past
short-lived habitats. Change accumulates languidly like
condensation. In the ancient sludge of existence,

        you

                disperse

                          endlessly.

MINT

Grandma played me her garden song
during the shallow heat of springtime.

She beat her palms against the soil,
caressed the dirt-laced scrapes on my knees.
Jewels of transcontinental sweat lined her bosom
as she hacked up furtive weeds.

Granny licked her peeling sugarcane lips
—they parted, & forth sprung an aria of flowers

There were whole land masses dropping from her hands,
breathing soul into fragrant coriander and parsley
ballads of San Juan & Mississippi, West Africa
reconciled in Sunday dew-kissed grass.

Look how the slender spines of lilac
bow to the sunflower's sullen crowns.
Just yards away, a squash blossom
swan song wanes towards summer.

She sat in the cool shade, mint leaves whistling,
her back creaking
like slave ships on salted ocean.
She's found ways to harvest her own skin

—ripe like wild bananas
slow & deliberate.

ON THE OUTSKIRTS OF EDEN

the white lady next door had such a beautiful apple tree
she defended with her life.
when squirrels tried to nibble

                                  on its garnet grace,
we would hear the pop pop of her grandson's bb gun,
discouraging their impish feast.

a squirrel without a tail survives—its equilibrium forever
distorted,
unable to balance on a tree's soft limbs, it chews on the half-rotted
apples littering the ground, risking blight for nourishment.

                     as children, we heeded her warning
so we waited for the branch to bend over our fence, heavy with
fruit, before flinging sharp pebbles as artful offerings,
tiny in their metamorphic launch to deliver precious harvest.
architects of freedom in our precision, we giggled as our makeshift
arrows struck through thin wood, sending sweet-fleshed jewels
into the soft embrace of our lawn.

                     my aunt once told me: laughter is the most
                     primal form of prayer.

we are all parishioners of mischief, of delight that stretches
beyond imposition.
i watched awestruck as my cousin turned her smiling face to the
sky,
opened her arms to catch what bounty has emerged after a long,
wilting season.
                     hands dusted with pollen, the green root of her
untendered,
she collected her God-given right, bit into a hardwon pleasure
full of spirit, still tailed, giggling with blossom-laden gospel.

LIFE CYCLE

america is a factory.
my father builds security cameras from discarded junk phones;
their cracked screens, subterranean stained glass
                              burgeoning blessings. come one, come
all if you dare.
he welds a fine line between surveillance & security. my father is
no stranger to a gun.
my father believes in a self-proclaimed rapture.
the hills have eyes. my father's lenses thicken as his
vision differs. defers. at the end of the world, he hopes to patent
his despair.

america is a landfill.
underwater, bloodline brined, it soured. my neighbor pours the
leftover liquid from a pot o' greens into his garden. billowing
green stink arises, stains room for ripening.
                              Black folks despise waste.
the last drops of Crown Peach in the dog's water bowl, for taste.
the plastic bags
under my auntie's kitchen cabinet, exceptional
cushioning for our endangered shadows. never afforded the
softness of packing peanuts. is the soul biodegradable? can it be
upcycled? at least we still have granny's house. wrap your
apparitions in polyester coves, send them out to ocean.
may they forever exist in sedimentary purgatory, float floating on.
                                        in this sense, we never rest.
                                        in this sense, pollution profits.
won't these white folks come and pick up the damn trash?

america is a false idol -- all my people iconoclasts.
look out the window at alladat. GATdamn. what is he protecting?
ain't nothing here ours but scraps of metal. melt it all down why
dontcha. some homes are worth less than their copper pipes,
this metallic stew pot boiling over. my ancestors bartered their
gold teeth for green,
earned heart disease & curdled cream dreams instead as the planet
warms another degree. momma says my degree won't save me.
s'pose Cash really does Rule Everything Around Me.

                                        i wonder—what rich
                                        bones can broth a new
                                        vanguard?

can a nigga get a witness?

america is a malignant tumor.
o how i long to capitalize this intrusion in our collective heart
                                            beat, beating
away at the floorboard of good senses until the spirits rattle
around, pushing daisies.
memory-stinging nettle, unsilenced. watch the good earth reclaim
clunkers4cash.
                        nostalgia makes a mockery of present.
                                the open-faced sores on my uncle's
                                knuckles, a tribute to this nation's
                                success.
i won't bullshit you. he reeks of burnt sienna & ember. it all reeks
of pirated pyrite. fool's gold. i talk too much about my
grandmother's hands because they threshed this country. great
migration granny—built Ford tough. a gorgeous ghost gnarled
into graphics. look closely: you can see flakes of calluses soldered
to your car's lithium battery. i talk too much about my
grandmother's hands because they became cracked by
bleach//ammonia//
                        everything meant to whiten and purge bacteria.
                        she passed down her genealogy of anguish, lead
                        hardened blood, black lung coughing up
                        embattled blues—wasn't the tin man once
                        chopping through scorched earth?
                                            my gut is filled with
                                            vengeful
                                            microorganisms.
                        today & everyday beyond grief, i throw my
                        grease against any surface
                        in need of shine.

america, define yourself a country *exactly*.
my offering: a knotted bellyache of sadness born beyond a
destined horizon,

manifested. the embers of our lost selves tumbling across the West
Coast.
even the mountains seem to collapse with sadness—the spine of
uninherited earth curved like that of a funeral wailer,
an assembly line aggravating access. all that rust corroding our
good sense.

                              riddle me this: how can i be well
                              when my lawn is forever burning?

9 INDIAN FRUIT OIL MONEY HOUSE BLESSING™

*"annancy [anansi] admirers will probably reply that in order to
cope with an unstraight and crooked world one needs unstraight and
crooked paths"* —Rex Nettleford

[1]the dead harmonize. invocations of one bring many—each
tongue a split cypher. scents stuck to southern summer steam: 9
fruits, virginia slims,
cat food, folgers, propane,
plastic wrapped furniture, old cognac, nail polish,

body heat,
the dead red of
summer.

ceiling fan blowing the same hot air around in circles.
DISCLAIMER: curio only.
[222] the Lord gon' bless me today! my bones look better at the end
of the world, cut off from flesh. a headless ghost, or, only a head
severed from ancestral body. obscure enough to let most anything
& everything in. clear as dishwater. don't we all just look the
same? *oh don't you know we got a lil bit of everything in us. can you
use some creative license? those memories are best kept in a lockbox
on the vanity*
[3] anansi learned to shapeshift by watching distorted tides of the
Atlantic. his long body—salt-stained. trickster-shorn skin,
patched together bloodline remnants for new regalia. fragrance
always signals a return, massages memory. roots stretching east
both planted//displanted. fruit from nowhere & everywhere at
once.
[4]when a culture is preserved, is it pickled? is it
smoked//frozen//vacuum sealed? does it lose its sazon in an effort
to prevent spoilage? does savagery stay put or just evolve with the
times? does the scent of God linger on our fingertips still?
[5]agua. propelente (A-55). fragrancia. estabilizadores.
conservadores. collapsed fruit stuck to dehydrated lineages—what
remains is diffusion.
[6]dispersed carcinogens intermingling. breath is a necessary
sacrifice to be had for a small blessing. golden ghastly spray.
borrowed time, anyways.

[7]mist modified for survival. the story changes every seaport,
canning culture. umbilical cords buried under provision grounds.
if we can't source, we invent. if we can't invent, we release to the

breeze time after time.

[8]there remains a fine line between enlightenment &
entertainment. we anointed our walls with the dead matter
behind our gums. eyes plugged//flushed dark by a landlord who
says he can only be responsible to what he sees.

[9]i disagree. in her final years, my greatmother's world didn't extend
beyond her porch. her eyesight wanes. she has seen enough.
incense smoke carries her blossoms eastward.

ACCESSING EXCESS

Goddamn! Baby you lookin' so fresh to death
What you finna do? Where you goin with all that gas?
Illustrious immaculate blk- ooooweeee! *Nigga, I'm tryna*
get like you, sew a whole seance to my gown & retrieve
forgotten gossip in silk & sateen of Biblical proportions!
O' my gorgeous glittering Gods of goodlooks all grown:
I mean, have you ever tasted sweetness from the source?
It's almost enough to make a nigga hop a flight and go
back to where loves him best: niggas doowopping a
silk press, aloe dipped loc, creases so sharp, starched to a soldier's
salute, return to a mouth of embodied pleasure, an adornment
ordained by centuries of hand me down joy, but *Bitch!*
Soon as that stimmy hit I drown myself in debauchery.
Look quick!
I'm a bead on Serena's hair at the 1998 US Open.
I'm the gold in yo granny's teeth.
I'm Smino's opal grill smoking swisher sweets.
I'm decadence for the sake of decadence alone!
Yes, me & my niggas be ungovernable/unquenchable,
over the top, extra, indulgent,
reinventing beauty one berry-stained thread at a time,
our wayward fantasies too grandiose to ever be appreciated by
the colonial machine of our scarcity myth nightmares.
Lord, look how we glow even in our grief—

                                            Baby, you can't clock
                               this crease!
Never doubt a nigga & a paycheck, a nigga & an advent speaking
all that is gaudy & sensual & demanding *I am here,*
I am aching to be seen.
True, I am extravagant—doesn't Earth Mother drench herself in
new color every season too? New shades pulled from a legacy of
green glamor: dare say my feet ain't planted somewhere, like I
ain't a product of transfer, transmutation, ecological
restructuring,
like i don't pray with the same hands i fold my garments with.
I am throttling the life out of miracles as I wring pain from
wet cloth—watch as I stretch culture beyond erosion.
Imma keep my fabrics I've earned my keep,
could teach you more about

sustainability than you could ever sermonize.
Cut from a different cloth, so I be
holding good flesh, just yearning to be free.

NATURE DOCUMENTARY

humans are the ringmasters of paradise.
problem is, these showmen cannot perform
without circusing the wandering black
bear of my heart.

NO NEUTRAL ZONES

at the playground, pretend is power.
children build brave new worlds from dirt & air, the
alchemy of self learned through the unspoken hierarchy
of the jungle gym. during the solstice, drought precluded
imagination. everyone so eager to cool off, shoes became
sticky with permissible color from melting paletas

so i, careless enough to sweat out a press n' curl to pursue
pleasure elsewhere, lent my hues to a make-believe apparatus.
in the dry grass, they wrote me out of their fantasy realms:
at the edge of paradise, there are no Black folks. i could be
a slave, but not a mermaid—a mule but not a dragon.
my hands so bruised the darkness blends the edges of my history.

we raced to the treetops, skinned knees straddling heaven
while the king of conifers lectured me on the historical
inaccuracies of my existence. below, a polyester flower memorial
stunk of piss & neglect, synthetic tributes to the sad-eyed boy
ended by a stray bullet, a painful reminder that they too were
encroaching on grief-stricken land.

i cried as the nearby HOA kids hung from the branches,
snapping bark from ancient trunks as their parents made plans
to uproot. the trees near the baseball field weren't just overgrown
wood gems but my cousins, though this relation also was too
fantastic to comprehend. meanwhile, the bars on the apartments
across the street reminded my bones what it means to be rusted.

once, a young boy pulled a box braid from my hair,
joked that if he planted it, *would a nigger sprout up from the soil?*
i laughed it off as i do most hurt, more worried about the
unfurling of my grandmother's artistry by white hands,
the same way an apathetic nurse smudged the letters on her birth
certificate, effectively erasing her first honor, a name.

the park, the neighborhood have both been remodeled—
like most, we had to sell to survive; everything changed but the
trees. the plastic roses in my grandmother's house are gathering
dust now, forever trapped in bloom. maybe it would be better to
have planted something that at least knew death as release.
the trees are losing their needles. they too are parched.

BLUSH HOTTENTOT

You do not need to search long to find nectar.
I know that honey is oozing out of inkwells—
                        though the sweet that I crave
may not taste the same on a different tongue.
Take the strawberry tree, whose flowers
produce a bitter honey but is still considered
a delicacy.
I can't be compared to another's ambrosia
lest I forget my own gifts.
                        From fragrance comes
perpetual longing, opaque in its multitudes.
I open mouth kiss the dark
& her plumwine lips return my flavor every time.
I'll be tender, only if the price is right.
Bonnet on crooked, magic mushroom of my mind
practicing Latin names like the bruised
flesh of mishandled fruit,
shadow spots emergent, revealing deep desire
to own what cannot be extracted without
care.

AUBADE FOR ROSEMARY EGGS

in a shared kitchen, you made me rosemary eggs
following a sun salutation of hungry love-making. I
watched the golden yolks pop under your gentle pressure,
center overflowing into margins, eager to fill the blackened
barrier of a cast iron pan with undeniable yellowness.
i wanted to burst like that, give way to my most sumptuous
flavor

persuaded by good heat; your thumb's firm kindness
releasing the dawn. for you i would be desperate, yolked, runny
darling with california eyes like wildfire, take me over,
burn my biomass to ash, fuel a stove to make eggs,
forever rosemaried.

Open, you say, lifting a fork to
my sunrise-stained lips &, just
like that,
all morning glory of me unfolds.

IV.
REBIRTH

THE ALIVENESS OF EVERYTHING BLACK &
BEYOND

he emerged

stardust

crystallized

in the euphoric

afterlife of

matter

he   mattered

from an
explosion

burst
cosmic

beacons

through collapse

abundance

sprang   forth

black was

(will be)

infinite

more than
stock of flesh

unmeasurable
   forget human
black was

beyond
that

every beginning
drew blood from his

stupendous

arch

each sunrise

birthed by
his evening womb
   before black

                    was black
he was love

& still after
because of
        his depths
        expanding

past the   margin
overtaking edges
                        dark space
                overflowing
diffused across
                        the celestial   abyss
in apocalypse's
                        dark aftermath

the stuff of gods
                        flowed
in   his
                                veins

look up
                        see
                        how the   moon
is but an ornament
                        nestled
    in the   cascading vapor

                        of life

WASPS

in 2020 it was discovered that wasps are bioindicators of heavy metals in industrial areas. the markings on their faces, usually overlooked by casual viewers, reveal phenotypic effects of metal pollution.[1]

it's no secret i came out my momma mad.
black striped & wrongly yellowed,
only recently i've begun to understand
the depths of my own anger, the vengeance
lingering like inheritance in my blood.
heavy metals such as lead & cadmium have
been proven to cause tremors, irritability—
"behavioral" issues environmentally
determined, geographically marred in markings,
defined by poison that creeps under my exoskeleton.
only god can judge me, but it seems as though
those crafted in his image seek annihilation
for me and mines, something quicker than
the lead-laced purgatory
they expect us to wallow in.

i do what comes naturally. the earth has
a long memory & i've built my dream palace
at the center of her toxic afterlife. i am
a pollinator of my own design, a mean boozer
buzzing around, fueled by fermented fruit;
nobody's friend, yet I do my own part to
remind other creatures what is lost when
green falls to gray. child of the rustbelt
blues, industry sullies my skin deep-silver.

---

[1]Skaldina, O., Ciszek, R., Peräniemi, S. et al. Facing the threat:

common yellowjacket wasps as indicators of heavy metal pollution. Environ Sci Pollut Res 27, 29031–29042 (2020).

https://doi.org/10.1007/s11356-020-09107-2

once, one of the good humans set a bowl of water
on his windowsill, the summer heat gasping
raw metal. i watched my kin collapse, drown in mercy.
these thirsty poor things desperate for relief beyond
neglect's quiet. fear streaks my face like war
paint. my melanin wanes with every death
note etched into an unviable seed. to be
Black is to weather toxic accumulation—
to be made an example, but never
deserving of a solution. i pray you never get
close enough to see the damage.

COUGH

"when white folks catch a cold,
Black folks catch pneumonia" —Black proverb

no incense, no browbeaten psalm, no sweat rice, no two for fifteen
dollar church pie, no ofrenda, no chicken feet, head, thigh, or
neck, no molten mural, no sacrifice, no menstrual blood, no
honey jar, no road opener, no pastor's pulpit, no garlic cloves, no
force against me yet suddenly prosperous, no holy water, no
voracious devotion, no dutty wine, hip twist or twerk, no five on
it, no black eyed peas in the eveningtime, no backyard switch, no
soap or sin

> can burn out this stink. call our demise
> collateral baptism. our lungs flush with the
> burden of dead dust. these days, i pay good
> money for breath with no return on investment.

FOR AUNT RUBYE

many years ago, humans believed
rubies contained droplets of Mother Earth's blood.
it was said that rubies were born of fire from heaven
and in their fervor, burned to reign sovereign over
the lymphatic system. a descendant of the earth
herself, ruby strengthened hearts by removing
what ails that delicate organ: betrayal, vanities, loss.

like my forebearers, i wear your heavenly protection
on my left side. heart of hearts, ashes to ashes, i could only trust
the phoenix & its multiple rebirths. our ancestors knew fire as a
detoxifier; a prescribed burn removes pests & disease, releases new
seeds eager for germination. new growth guarding the old
until the old gives its ancient body back to dust.

a few years before your return to eternity, a
son of sharecroppers showed me to line the
topsoil with crystals. he grew by the moon's
patient cycle, unlearning everything about production
taught to him by a rent check. a glutinous freeholder
grandma left me a plot of land & you left me the wisdom
needed to sow gemstones from its fertile womb, your memory
cascading among the clouds, shouting *look upward, sistren!*

PORCH

"I keep a shotgun in every corner of my bedroom, and the first cracker even looks like he wants to throw some dynamite on my porch, won't write his mama again."

—Fannie Lou Hamer

I keep a piece of myself on the porch.
Don't test me. I have had everything ripped from my flesh
& still fix my gums to smile at those who wish me harm.
Don't try it. I am a nigga who comes from niggas & as such
I do not play. This body owns nothing—exists everywhere. You
can't kill me. All the fullness in the world collides within my
frame. A grand unraveling weathers me mighty vengeful: can you
say the same? My love shatters anything that has tried to cause me
harm. Ceremony predates survival, so leave my flowers at the
doorstep & dance until your heart bursts into a thousand new
iterations of Godliness. Fill my cup with lilac wine where one can
pull a Nina croon through the window until a swansong of rage
fills the walls & covers me in honeysuckle rose. Give me all that I
desire or nothing at all. I want a new wig. I want a plot of land. I
want a small win that carries me through the rest of forever.
I am owed at least that.

CONJURE WOMAN AFTER APOCALYPSE
c. 2020

the blood don't lie.   the blood hurt good.

           the blood is the only thing

we ever understood.   i wept a joyless conjure.

           the blood held a haint.

the blood stay on the stoop.   i wish mosquitoes

        peace elsewhere.   this blood

                   been

tainted.   i sleep on a mat on the veranda.   i boil

     my thighs

               in the sun.   rest

comes in afterbirth.   i freed an entire

bloodline   hooked to   my flesh.

      blood don't no tall tales.

my progeny   liberated themselves

     through my wounds.

no eve of mine   shapeshifts me.

     stillborns slither

in the weeds of my namesake.

               i let them ask

questions.   let them chase.

           they

ran towards ruinous light.   nobody wan' remit to

dark.   i stood

zombified.   stuck in sun-stained purgatory.

      the body: a peril and a possibility.   i a mythology.

                              guilt stricken flesh.

return to tree.   mirror dust.

                              return to breath.

the dead don't tell   no false tales.

      the dead don't sleep.

this country don't   know sanctity.

      it know spillage.

          know blood.   how

easily they let it

        spoil.

ALLOTMENT

The Dawes Act of 1887 fragmented communal indigenous
territory in Oklahoma into individual allotment plots. Water
ran clay red as the crust of the earth dissolved into splintered
versions of itself. The squatters who came before//after renamed
land solid muscle. Big Ag lurked in the shadows, sowing
genetically modified seeds of seizure. A former slave-driver stood
guard with a gun. Cultures carried on the fat backs of bees,
dispersed in silence. Meanwhile, someone tried to loot our piece
of fallow.

History unfolded like a moth-eaten quilt. The Five Tribes sought
to ban previously enslaved Black citizens from owning territory.
The Black face of the Native is a ghost story no one wants to tell.
The Black face of the Native crumbled like overworked terrain,
never to be seen again.

My blood runs thick with fractured histories,
                                        wholly made up
by those tribes of the West African Coast,
rendered unfamiliar. American—
some broken definition.
                              I am built of fragmentation.
What allotments compose my skin?
Everywhere I go I am a squatter; the land
does not recognize my city slicker feet,

                all my kinship cast out to the Atlantic,

        swimming towards any bit of home
this world can spare me.

                                        I turn

my patchwork brown face
                towards the sun,
                                try on ancestors like

old clothing,
                unsure of which ones will fit.

PLOSIVE FOR DENVER
"Queen city of the Plains; for in you we live, and are loved."
- Ted Vaca

Denver, my devil dear didn't you defeat yourself from jump?
didn't you define yourself from get? dios mi', damned by
definition, deliciously divine, done tempted me to stay dry
Dixieland. darling Denver, didn't you debut dutifully? deep
durazno summertime skies, dandelion debauchery dominated by
delight. Denver, you are a desperate decomposer. didn't you warn
me of my own deflowering? diminishing daydreams, dour
drought, a damaging city's deception persists. dedicated OGs
discerned your domingo deliverance, doping your devotees due to
deceitful decolonization, demented dualities dished daggers
desired by development. yet so dynamic & dreamy: delinquents
dangle from your dreads, disastrous in your delectability. Denver, i
dance with you at a distance. displacers disturb deities, denote
dents in your dirty, dim dusk. so drunk you are in your delusion,
dawg; Denver wears a dashiki to a jazz festival, decides herself
dapper. discordant chords demolish pipe dreams. Denver
dayflower, don't demarcate me deadweight. i wiped my shoes on
your dank doormat. your decay stuck to my digits. deracinated by
damnable design. dear Denver, don't disregard my diatribes. it's
my duty to disparage your disappearing decision.

your dispossessed have come to collect their debt.

CHROMATIC

Grandma was a mother, a hairdresser, a beautician, a stylist, an opera singer, a church-goer, a God-fearing Christian, a cook, a pastry chef, a bad bitch, a freedom fighter, a conscientious objector, an ass-whupper, a Southern belle, a great grandmother, a wife, a widow, a scholar, a gardener, a loud mouth, a bad mamajama, a panther, a misogynist, a feminist, a giant, a misnomer, an Elton John fan, a soap opera enthusiast, a recipe hoarder, a librarian, the alpha and the omega, a PYT, a glass house, a Black supremacist, a mess, a negress, a shit talker, a bra burner, a seamstress, a gossip, a migrant, a butcher, a baker, a candlestick maker, a seamstress, an aesthetician, a union.
Look how she glow, she glow, she glow. Look how she keeps glowing, glows.

Grandma wants to move back to her true home in Wayne County. Besides, there aren't many Black folks in Denver & the ones who are here are a lil too weird, they smell like patchouli & free love & all the things that could get us killed. The niggas in the northside whistle from lowriders & sport neck tattoos—the difference is, the hands that pull the trigger will be the same color as the ones that layer on the dirt, that will press the wounds into submission, that will clutch pearls & beat on the congregation pews & wipe tears & snot & fry fish in thick cast iron pans & break branches for switches & sing LOVE & RAGE.
My mother. My mother says
do you see?
Do you see why I am telling you this?
Do you see how Detroit,
no matter where I be,
Detroit forever lives, lives on
in me?

REFRAIN

Detroit, lauded as a truly American art form,
birthed from the underbelly of resistance i.e.
Black joy, broke its back somewhere along the way,
or was tripped, stood up,

bamboozled, deleted its history, crawled back out the den
to face a new audience.
Now Spectacle, no longer spectator, no longer musician,
no longer owner or steward.

Mama goes back to Detroit & starts reminiscing,
conjuring old ghosts. It is not hard to summon
memory on this land—
the dead here do not engage in games of trickery
& shadow, they demand to be heard,

hammering their heads against the concrete—
the concrete speaks in crumble, all the potholes
dark chasms, filled by an everlasting desire to claim a home.
Aunt Janice sewed this city together, Cousin Lazerick worked

these factories, all the ancestors bones
are scattered across this landscape. From Dearborn Heights
to Anchor Bay, our blood greases every wheel turning the damn
car. We are the damn car, bitten by the smoke, rust and risk of
removal.
Look right here, this street
—that's where Aunt Selma & Aunt Lump used to live.
That lot used to be a park.
There might still be chestnut trees.

RETURN. RETURN. RETURN.
after Richard Wright

I'm running further West in pursuit of hard-won
greens. I'm greedy for an enduring bloom, insatiable
in my desire to reclaim a culture beyond
the eroded coast of conquest. What greets me?
The Pacific, another chasm. known, but unfamiliar
its visage changes with the seasons & here I am both
squatter & homesteader—
green guardian marred by industry.
Humidity overwatered me, now I crave that
arid spring to desiccate my exit wounds—
yes, there will be drought. Heartache too, though
who can say the longing for rain isn't the same as
the desire for a crisp blues note to soothe the soul into
darker revolution?
True, I came to oil the shipyards with my name,
to raise up my dry acres with cropland, to slash, burn &
build once more.
I cannot outrun the South, her memory stays
stuck to my skin the same way wild garlic
lingers on the tongue. Sun-stained blackberry body
reminiscent of fullness to be had, elsewhere.

ACKNOWLEDGEMENTS

This is a book that would not be made possible without a village. When I first sought out to unravel the intricate threads of ecology, culture, heritage and memory, I first turned to my family albums. There, I was reminded of the many relations (biological and chosen). In continuing with this gratitude for relation, I am indebted not only to my family (Lucas & Carters), but to the elders who stepped up and helped cultivate my curiosity for nature, science, creative expression & exploration: Nii-Akwei Allotey, Ms. Sarah Rainey, Aunt Lejeune, Mr. Harrison (rest in heaven), Mr. Charles Henry, Ferdinand Fiofori (rest in heaven), and all the OGs at the City Park tennis courts. I am especially grateful to my Uncle Waverly and Aunt Nena who demonstrated innovation and dynamism in their own art practice & continue to mentor me as an independent Black artist navigating this world.

I extend a huge thank you to many wonderful educators, including East High School's "Llama Mama" Ms. Connelly who signed me up for my first Slam. Subsequently, special thanks is owed to Ken Arkind, Suzi Q. Smith, Magni McDonough, Assétou Xango, Rebecca Preston, Franklin Cruz, and all others involved in Minor Disturbance (NO BEDTIME!) for opening a whole new world of creative expression for this young weirdo. Everything was given to God and to the 303. Thank you for Five Points, its unwavering memory and for 300 days of sunshine.

For your guidance in weaving together my shared interests of environment and storytelling, I am grateful to Dr. Shifra Sharlin, Dr. Sigma Colon, Sarah Stillman, Dr. Dorceta Taylor, Dr. Stephanie LeMenager, Dr. Duygu Avcı, Dr. Verlyn Klinkenborg, Dr. Carol Carpenter, Dr. AND Mayor Justin Cummings (what!!), Dr. Erika Zavaleta, Heather Smith, and the incomparable Claudia Rankine. For providing me the space and support to fully be myself and bring every aspect of my wild, talkative, Gemini self to our meetings, retreats and performances, thank you very much to the many members of WORD: Spoken Word at Yale.

Many thanks to Tin House, UC Berkeley's Poetry for the People Climate Activism Residency, the Soupbone Collective, the Watering Hole and Just Buffalo Literary Center for supporting my work.

For reading first drafts, honing editing skills and just chopping it up about all things life & writing, my endless gratitude to Arty Pineda, Sidney Saint-Hilaire, Irene Vazquez, Aya de Leon and Alexis Aceves Garcia.

And of course to literary ancestors Toni Morrison, June Jordan, Lucille Clifton, Wanda Coleman, Toni Cade Bambara, Zora Neale Hurston, Octavia Butler, James Baldwin, bell hooks, and Ntozake Shange. An immense gratitude to all of the Black creative ancestors who held the stories in their hearts and under their tongues when written word was too dangerous to venture.

Thank you to my mother, whose work ethic and visionary spirit I have long admired and learned from.

And lastly, I lift my hands in praise of Earth Mother, whose water fed the plants harvested to bind these pages, whose trees gave body to this text, whose minerals set words upon the page. In celebration of the mountains, of the plains, of the blossoms and buds, of the river and the sea, of the soil, the forest, the sand, the green goodness that sustains us all. May we continue to heal our relationship to you and relearn the ancestral ways of doing right by you.

POEMS PREVIOUSLY PUBLISHED IN EARLY STAGES

Landfill (Foglifter Press)
collards (Frontier Poetry)
God Save the Forest (Five South Magazine)
a black hair study in commensalism, i.e. grease and glory in the marshlands of my scalp (Isele Magazine)
Running (World Literature Today)
i still won't get my hair wet (Flyway Journal)
the plug won't (ClavMag)
meditations on sweetness and other fruits (Thimble Lit Magazine)
Ode to the Spirit of Left Eye (Already Felt Journal)
blackest blue (formerly deep sea diving in Women's Studies Quarterly: Black Love)
Nameless (Lumiere Review)
durag (Southern Humanities Review Auburn Witness Poetry Prize Finalist)
Life Cycle (2022 Great River Review Pink Poetry Prize Finalist)
Accessing Excess (Blackbird Press News & Review)
porch (Apogee Journal)
Allotment (Michigan Quarterly Review)
Chromatic (Hennepin Review)
refrain (Flyway Journal)

ABOUT THE AUTHOR

Ashia Ajani is a sunshower, a glass bead, a product of desire, an overripe nectarine. Ajani is a multi-genre environmental storyteller & educator hailing from Denver, CO, Queen City of the Plains and the unceded territory of the Cheyenne, Ute, and Arapahoe peoples. Ajani is a lecturer in the African American Studies Department at UC Berkeley and a climate resilient schools educator and researcher with Mycelium Youth Network. A recipient of fellowships and support from Tin House, Just Buffalo Literary Center, The Watering Hole and Winter Tangerine, Ajani believes in the possibility of Black insurgent knowledge to weather the climate crisis. A Black future is happening, always.

ashiaajani.com

If You Like Ashia Ajani, Ashia Likes...

Lessons on Being Tenderheaded
Janae Johnson

This Way to the Sugar
Hieu Minh Nguyen

Counting Descent
Clint Smith

Divine Divine

Brandon Wint

Amulet
Jason Bayani

Write Bloody Publishing publishes and promotes great books of poetry every year.
We believe that poetry can change the world for the better. We are an independent press
dedicated to quality literature and book design, with an office
in Los Angeles, California.

We are grassroots, DIY, bootstrap believers. Pull up a good book and join the family.
Support independent authors, artists, and presses.

Want to know more about Write Bloody books, authors, and events?
Join our mailing list at

www.writebloody.com

WRITE BLOODY BOOKS

CPSIA information can be obtained
at www.ICGtesting.com
Printed in the USA
JSHW020304040423
39877JS00003B/204